# (You Broke Me) Open

# (You Broke Me)
# Open

BRYNN TAYLOR

BROOKLYN, NY

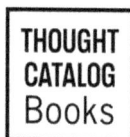

*To the boys I've loved, the friends
I've held on to, and the family I
owe my life to.*

*You have created
me and are part of
everything that
I create.*

———————————

*I carry your heart
I carry it in my heart.*
*—E. E. Cummings*

# For The Readers

Take this book with you
wherever you may go,
And my hope is that
you can reach far more
than your destination

# CONTENTS

# Introduction

I always tried to write my ending before my story began
or go back and write a few more pages
to make it all seem more beautiful,
and worthy of some literary prize

My diary was always filled with half-truths
I hoped nobody would see how spineless I was
But people always slipped right through my gutter
and ran their fingers along my empty pages

My case for as long as my shelves were vacant
was to fill each new chapter with an extraordinary tale
as emotionally satisfying as a romance novel
and more magical than fantasy

In my imaginary universe the setting was in your arms
and the plot thickened in your heart
just like I had always dreamt it
from the moment I began writing
to the moment my pen filled with your ink

I asked you to end it all before it even began
but the story we wrote was not at all
like the fictitious one I had planned

Now your ink has mixed with mine,
and these words are all I have of us
to put up on the shelf and leave behind

Life is becoming more of a reality

If you open a cover, before you are ready
or write an impossible ending
you watch it become a tragedy

# Warning

Who I was
before you
has been
shattered

You may be
cut by these
broken pieces
I have scattered

# Cleaning Out the Closet

There are many things that I outgrew,
Like my favorite pair of jeans (and you)

A dress I wore when we went away
You told me you fell in love that day

The shirt I wore when I met your mom
Mother's Day was the day you moved on

A sweater you gave me when I was cold
I wept as I slept in a pile of old, folded clothes

I gave them away because of how quickly I grew
or maybe because they reminded me of you

# Before You

I frequently tended
to the soil in my heart
so that one day
I could cultivate a
garden

Then I wondered why
I appeared so lush
to those with deserted
souls

*Men tumbled in like weeds*
*But you were the fruits of my labor*

# Queen

Her smile was a drawbridge
perfectly hinged
that would lower for sweet talk
to draw people in

Her castle with towers
unusually high,
But her thick walls weren't so menacing
when you looked in her eyes

# Tidal Wave

My heart was always big but
I was careful who I gave it to
Always cautiously selective
Until it decided upon you
Going into my own sanity
Hoping there was more
Waiting for your tidal wave
To brush up on my shore

## Darkness Falls

Everyone saw how beautiful you were in the light
But it was in the dark that I fell in love with you

# Heaven

I was crying out
Clawing at my shell
Rotting inside
My own personal hell
Nobody listened
Nobody could see
Until your gates of hell opened
But oh, they looked like
heaven to me

# The Art of Broken Pieces

You were attracted to
the gold in my heart

I couldn't tell you
it was only there

*to fill in the cracks*

# The Day We Met

It all traces back to that
one unassuming day
I remember your smile
how it blew me away
I remember talking
but very little was said
So little to prepare me
for what lay ahead

# Breathe

Our love could only
be described as every breath
that makes you feel alive

# Once in a Blue Moon

The night was July 31, 2015
A rare blue moon to set the scene
We met and it was like a dream,
so wonderfully unforeseen

# Made in Heaven

Me, so young and impressionable
And you, with the best first impression
The stars must have perfectly aligned
For we were a match made in heaven

# The Start

I loved you in a moment
it happened instantly
Your dominating presence
had quickly captivated me
I became weak at the knees
Or maybe weak at the heart
I didn't know how to love you
But I was ready to start

# Selective Hearing

We saw each other
Beyond what others saw
Freeing a whirlwind of feeling
So unbelievably raw
My finger on the trigger
Butterflies in my stomach
It didn't matter what anybody said
I never thought anything of it

# Chlorine

You pulled me closer in your pool
and in that moment I felt so light
as if I was incapable of drowning

I would've given you my heart
right then and there, but I was
afraid to dive into shallow water

# My Best Mistake

Before you, I was wild
I would say that I was blind
Making all the best mistakes
Living outside of my mind
You'd say that I was crazy
But I have zero regrets
Of all the boys who played me
You were my best mistake yet

# Poker

I tried my hand at love before
Always playing with the cards I was dealt
Going off of luck and the rush
Life had finally upped the ante
My darling, you were a royal flush

# Hypnosis

Your father told me how lucky I was.
You wouldn't remember that day,
much unlike the way it so vividly sticks out in my mind.

But I remember I was looking right at you.
And I could feel everyone else's eyes,
patiently waiting for my humble reply.

I didn't need a reminder,
although I smiled at his jest.
Because each moment I spent with you
I knew that I was truly blessed.

Forgive me for if I seemed surprised,
but it's because I was so hypnotized.

# The End

You told me that was it
You said I was the end
The words sounded so lovely
For awhile,
It was nice to pretend

# Compliant

It didn't take me long to see
That your love was killing me
You always had to be defiant
And wanted someone more
Compliant

# Your Gift to Me

He spoke of loyalty and devotion
In two words, he pried my heart wide open
For love and loyalty are the perfect gifts
But not when they force you to submit

# Paradox

Bound inside your paradox
of never speaking enough and
always having too much to say;
I was screaming words
in my head, but all I could hear
was the faint echo
inside your hollow cave

# Red Flags

Perhaps if red
wasn't associated
with passion
and love

We'd stop playing
with fire and
hazardous
chemicals

# Law of Attraction

He told me if he kept on loving me that we would eventually
hate each other.
I pondered for a while, wondering what that meant.
I couldn't imagine hating someone I loved every bit of.

He was afraid. He was telling me we wouldn't live up to each
other's expectations, but I didn't have any. I loved him
unconditionally. I forgave him for every mistake, while he
held me accountable for mine.

Eventually he did hate me because his life was a paradigm of
exceedingly high expectations and I was just the next one for
his ego to check off the list.

It was the moment he told me we'd end up miserable that he
flipped over the hourglass. But still, I could never hate him. I
just feel sorry that he'll always end up being right, and never
understand why.

# Tick-Tock

Always coming second
To the second hand on the clock
Maybe I'll come first
The day that time stops

# Lemonade

You always made
me lemonade and
I thought it was
to quench my thirst

But then when
I would ask for
some, you always
seemed to drink it first

# When The Roof Caved In

Your heart was my home
Until the roof caved in
And the very foundation
You based our love on
Collapsed beneath my feet

# Losing Control

I hope one day someone tells you
that they'll never leave you
and then slowly starts to pull the rug
out from underneath you
I hope your heart stops when they say,
"You'll always be mine."
and never starts back up when they run,
leaving you behind
I hope they say all these beautiful,
becoming words to fill your soul
and then they take them all away,
so you'll finally know the pain
of
losing
all
control

# Caged

Two love birds
sitting in a tree
I never saw a cage
'til you were
begging to be free

# Shut Down

You say that nothing ever heals
But think about how it feels
To try to talk and fix what's broken
Always getting shut down
When you try to be open

# Brick Walls

You were breaking down my walls
And brick by brick by brick
Building your own fortress

# Car Rides

I remember taking
long car rides
in the rain

The pounding on
the windshield
masking the
silence of
our pain

# Aisle Be Seeing You

His visions of the altar
Were so clear in his head
Was it that he altered his mind
Or never meant what he said?

# Losing My Mind

My mind shuts down when things get hard
But always forgets to tell my heart

# Madness

I knew it wouldn't last
But the thought of losing you
Drove me mad
I held on so tightly
With all the strength I had
You pushed me to my limit
But I knew I could do more
You mistook me for a quitter
And I never was before

# Cold-blooded

I wanted so badly
to resolve your pain
to warm up
whatever cold blood
was injected into
your veins

# Healers

I will never know what it's like
To turn someone away

I will never know what it's like
To not ask someone to stay

I will never know what it's like
To not look at you and cry

I will never know what it's like
To not even bat an eye

Can you tell me what that's like?
Can you tell me how it feels?

Because I don't think I'll ever know
How to not reach out and heal

# What Are You So Afraid Of?

You told me, "I don't like to be lonely"
Yet you were always alone
Searching for answers
You never found on your own
I could see through your pain
Like a sad cry for help
It was the moment I realized
You were afraid of yourself

# Captive Innocence

When I saw your baby picture
I melted; your face looked the same
All of your adorable innocence
captured in that one little frame
I sadly wished your heart could be
the same as then, too,
but I knew exactly what
this world had done to you.

# Retribution

It's still unclear what your true colors are
So much of you is seeking retribution
For your once broken heart

# Fermented

You've filled your hollow heart
With intoxicating waste
For everyone to drink and
I'm sure they'll love the taste
But those spirits have become your soul
And who you were is gone
I think you have been drinking
The distilled liquid
Of your fermented mind
For far too long

# Corrosion

Your examples of love were all toxic
And I guess so were mine
But that shaped me into a lover
Since I've seen how the heart can die

# Sink Her

You needed my heart
So I gave it to you
To borrow
Always wondering
If you'd give it back tomorrow
I knew I couldn't save you
But I took a leap of faith
Casting my love out on the line
Waiting for you
To take the bait

# Dig Deeper

I began
to dig up
the dirt in
your heart
that I spotted

I didn't see
the mounds
next to the
two graves
that you plotted

# Bleeding Out

If I knew you were
bleeding out
I never would have
nursed your wounds

# Narcissism

I still loved you after all the times you shut me out
After all the drinking, the cursing, and the lying,
and the times you left me dying
I still felt every single touch,
I could tell you loved me
Oh, so much

I guess looking back it's easy to see,
that love you had was more
an extension of you, and less for me,
and the day you chased me crying,
when I thought you would start trying
you were more afraid of losing yourself,
as if you couldn't see anyone else

Thinking "I love you," meant adoration, but yours
was a search for gratification

# Shades

You were my favorite
shade of blue but the
only colors you see
are black and white

# Nothing Left

"Be strong,"
I told myself
Because he needs
you to be

But what's going to happen
When I have nothing left
For me?

# In Your Hands

I have, too often, put myself
into the hands of someone else
Just praying their grip wouldn't
be too tight, but between your
fists, I could hardly put up a fight

# High Honor

You want people to fight for your affection
And only if they're worthy, do you accept them

Oh darling, even at your best
I bet you couldn't pass your test

# Tag, You're It

I'd let you win
Pretend it was a game
Let you point your finger
So you had someone to blame

When life came down on you,
You came down on me,
Never knowing what I'd get
Like a game of Hide and Seek

—

*The words "too much" escaped his lips*
*and I knew he meant it as an insult, but I*
*don't know who it hurt more, him or me.*

*"You are too much," he said, because he knew*
*he couldn't give me what I wanted. I began*
*to weep uncontrollably, trying to fight it.*

*I said, "Maybe I can ask for less from you."*

*"Maybe we should just take things at your pace."*

*"I know I can be too much, you're right."*

*The thing is, I am too much. I believe in the*
*good of people too much. I fight for what I*
*want too much. I care too much when I see*
*people give up. I want too much for the*
*people who want nothing for themselves.*

*I wept because I knew I had an impossible choice to make;*

*To leave and keep fighting for what I wanted,*
*or to be less of myself for the only boy*
*I ever wanted to fight with*

# Proceed with Caution

I saw you surrounded
by broken hearts
and broken bottles

I slipped through your
caution tape to try and cure
your fatal disease

# Look Away

I knew I could
see people
for who they
really were
but I refused
to look deep
into their
harsh realities

So I stayed
nearsighted
because the
only quick fix
for cock-eyed
optimism is
rose-colored
glasses

# Sensitive Soul

I did my best to
handle you with care
Your sensitive soul
is so very rare
But asking you
to open up
isn't abuse
I was asking you
to put your soul
to better use

# Blame Game

He asked me why I blamed him
for the downfall of our love
but he didn't understand
where the pain was coming from

I knew why I was angry
but I don't know how he couldn't see,
that although I knew his faults
I placed the blame on only me

We were so naïve and
I should've known the consequence
of putting my heart into the hands
of such incompetence

It's not his fault he couldn't love me;
his life was pretty artless,
and still, I never blamed him
one small bit for being heartless

# Tormented

I know you want to opt out
To hit the road alone
Blame everyone around you
And say you're better on your own
I know they weigh you down
The worries in your head
Locked in solitary confinement
So the torment doesn't spread

# Holding On

Ignoring the pain
I tried to understand
All the while knowing
I'd be holding your hand
I really should've left
That day you kicked me out
But I wanted to believe you
Even when I had my doubts

Still, I couldn't doubt you
Even when I knew I should
Through all the sleepless nights
I fought to see the good
I saw the hills of love
Behind the clouds of fear
You were all that mattered
So I fought back all the tears

# Nobody

If nobody was there for you,
was I no one when I cared for you?

# My Tears are Taunting Me

Trying, then crying
and as each salty
droplet rolled
off my chin,
silently they'd
say, "He wins."

# Stay

I saw it in your face
The moment you gave up
You couldn't look into my eyes
And say I was enough
And I knew it even more
When you began to pull away
Did you do those hurtful things
To make it hard for me to stay?
Or was it just because
you knew I wasn't leaving
either way?

# Game. Set. Match.

It wasn't much of a rally
as the ball was mostly
in your court

I had love on my side
but that gave me
zero points

*in our love game*

# Fool For You

Your love has rules
But I'm the fool
I play your games
And always lose

—

Now I was drowning in
your pool of insecurities,
and I dreamt of the moment
I felt so light in your hands.

— *it feels like ages ago*

# My Mistake

Eventually it got me
I started to lash out
I hated who I was
Waiting for love
Like rain in a drought

You waited for your golden moment
The chance you had to take
Waiting for me to slip up,
so you could tell me my mistake

# Your Love Was a Competition

Your sense that something better was out there became known
And that's when I realized...I would rather be alone

# The Price Isn't Right

If the prize for winning your love
Is getting to take care of you
For the rest of my life
While you leave a trail of breadcrumbs
For me to feel less hungry
Then I would rather starve

# The First Goodbye

I guess I should've figured
After the awful things we did
That someone had to stop it
But I just ran and hid
I hid behind my fears
You hid behind the lies
I'm glad you left me when you did
I'm just mad you said
the first goodbye

# Late Night Thoughts

Thoughts of you came late at night
To stroke my hair and whisper in my ear
I started to have nightmares
And you slowly started to disappear
Thank goodness for the daydreams
For love and for the sun
If I spent my life in darkness
I almost think I would succumb

# The You You Were

It was fitting for you to
disappear without a word
I had written letters upon letters
to try and make things work

You told me all I ever did
was tell you you were wrong,
but I just wanted the you
you were before you were
withdrawn

# Moving On

I tried to move on
To love other guys
I tried to get past
The hate and the lies
But the more I thought about it
The more I wanted you there
Were you going to try to fight for me?
Did you ever really care?

# Man in My Mind

Some days I think I'm doing great
But then I'm reminded of your face
As if life wants me to see you one more time
And fall in love with the man
You are in my mind

# Imagine

Imagine how different
things might be
If you had found yourself
before you found me

# Return to Sender

I licked the stamps
Signed on the dotted line
Sent the invitation
To try one more time

I waited for your answer
So don't say I didn't try
The message was received
I never got your reply

—

*I wanted him to feel guilty for everything he did*
*so that I wouldn't have to.*

*Why should he be the one allowed to move on*
*when I'm over here, taking all the blame?*

*But in reality, that isn't anyone's responsibility.*

*Just because I thought I was right*
*doesn't mean I had to tell him he was wrong.*

*Just because my integrity told me he was at fault*
*doesn't give me the right*
*to wave my finger at him.*

*He hurt me,*
*but reminding him doesn't change his behavior,*
*it only enhances his guilt.*
*So do I dangle the sword over his head*
*just so it doesn't fall on mine?*

*No, I just move out of the way.*

# Perfume

I used to want
to bottle up
your smell,
your warmth,
your touch,
reminding me
that I was loved
I could never
have enough

But now if I could
bottle you up
I'd keep you
under my bed.
I'd rather be
without your love
then let you
hurt someone
again

# When Love Runs Out

I am here because
one of us had to show up
and it wasn't you

## Too Little, Too Late

I wanted an apology,
but out of the prolonged silence
rose such a long-winded chase
for the acknowledgment of my pain
that sorry didn't cut it when sorry finally came

—

~~If I acted differently~~
~~What if~~
~~I could've just said~~*

*Don't re-write
the ending
Just keep going

# Small Victories

You think this is winning
but what did you achieve just
by being the first one to leave?

You can have your cake and eat it, too
and lead your life with greed
Take your small victories
I don't need them to succeed

# Check Mate

Sorry was his diversion
A calculated move of his pawn
to put others in check,
and escape from
the emotionally unpleasant

If only my guilt was
so easily redirected,
the distress and pain of others
could be used as a tactic
to protect my solitude

and I'd be good at chess

# I Thought The World Of You

I would've given you the world
You never thought you deserved

# I Couldn't Wait

I couldn't wait for you
as you kept my heart locked up
collecting dust

Contained and chained
until you resolved
your pain

Because outside of
your chamber
is a meadow

Where my heart
can grow and if
I throw away the key

I'll never know

—

*And then it clicks, and you finally see*
*life may never be the same again*
*but that is when you're truly free*

# Waste of Time

I always cared what others thought
A habit I should have broken
Your opinion mattered to me most
And you were so outspoken
I think I learned my lesson
With my self-worth on the line
Letting you define me
Was a colossal waste of time

# Final Notice

Ours is a book you cannot renew
I held on for as long as I could
but now it's way overdue

# More Sure

It broke me at first
We had so much promise
I thought of the days
When we were so honest
I had been disappointed
Plenty times before
But this was a different kind of let down
Because I never felt more sure

# Flashbacks

Now when I think of you
It's nothing but a montage
Of you caressing my hips
And stroking your ego

# Timing Is Everything

She asked me, "When do you
write your best poems?"

As I looked up to find the answer
I was reminded of the days I used
to sleep beside you. Every time I
woke up in the middle of the night
I had your warm and tender body
to slowly caress me back to sleep.
Now when I'm taunted by these
memories, I wake up and all I have
is a blank piece of paper and pen.

"When I'm alone," I said.

# Storm

Perhaps because my mind is so clouded
by you, I struggle knowing whether I'll
cause too much of a storm with my words

—

"Love happens when you least expect it."

*I don't know how much I buy that.*
*Love is not an involuntary action. It's not*
*something that just happens unconsciously.*
*You can fall in and out of love when you*
*aren't looking. I get that. And I know that*
*sometimes you can't help who you love if*
*that person has become a part of you.*
*But I never met anybody and instantly*
*told them I love them. I always wait until the*
*perfect moment so that I can deliberately*
*proclaim that that person has stolen my*
*heart, but I won't do so until I have carefully*
*assessed exactly what that means to me.*

*If someone has told you lately that they*
*just fell out of love with you, then I really*
*believe they didn't know what that love*
*meant to begin with.*

# The Challenge

I always said I wanted someone who challenged my mind.
Someone who gave me a reason to try harder so that
I would become a better person.

You challenged me every single day.
You told me my feelings weren't valid
so I had to try to hide them.

Each time I spoke up was an opportunity for debate,
and I had to quickly find a way to come to a resolution
when you inevitably disagreed with every word I said.

I guess it was a good thing—you making me try so hard.
And eventually, I did become a better person for it.

But it took me a long time to figure out,
that the challenge wasn't to get you to see my truth.
It was to make myself see, *that I don't need you to.*

—

I thought you were the glue
keeping me together

Turns out you were just the
chain tying me to your hitching post

*—Until I broke free*

# Fossils

You can hide the memories
But I'll be forever imprinted
On your soul, and my name forever
Carved in your bones

## The Last Fool I Loved

One day I'll meet the man
Who makes you look like a fool
For giving me up

But until then,
You're just the last fool
I loved

# Delusion

Our love was a delusion
made up of the fear in
our hearts that revealed
the truth about ourselves

# Change

People can
handle change
until we notice the
harmful parts of ourselves
we fear other people see
and we begin to think
that is all we'll ever be;
it's those of us who
accept those parts
who begin to
break free

# Mirrors

We would get ready in front of your bathroom mirror
and when you saw my finished face, you'd
always tell me I was beautiful

I loved the way you noticed all the times I
wanted to look good for you

And the way you pointed out when I
would try a little too hard

It's wonderful when I broke free
how I saw the beauty
that you and the mirror
couldn't see

# Happiness

Happiness used to be
standing by your side
But now I find happiness
in just being alive

# Our Story

I hear you don't
like how I've been
telling our story

Discrediting my words
and making them
sound more ordinary

Pardon my darling
but those words are a
tribute to the
performance you gave

You wanted to be
the tragic hero
now all of your
world
is
a
stage

# Buried Treasure

Her ocean is so deep
so that those who only
conquer shallow water
are not gallant enough
to swim to the bottom
of her conscious and see
the treasures hidden
in the darkest places
of her soul

# Empty-Handed

I came up empty-handed
so many times, but now
I have a pen in my hand and
all these words in my mind

# My Sanity

I am insane
and sane
all rolled
into one

Fragile,
Easily
undone

I unravelled
and wished
I would've
stayed spun

Now I'll give
up my sanity
for no one.

# Poet Tree

Plant me in the ground
and I will grow branches
in all different directions

Cut me down before
my story is finished and
I will rip off the flyleaves
and fill them with poetry

# The Beautiful Side of Our Love

I could write about the beautiful
side of our love

Write how every word that ever
escaped your soft and supple
lips sent an ocean's ripple through
me, entrancing my worrisome mind

Write about each and every
moment your dazzling smile
sent moonbeams into my heart from
across a dark and crowded room

Write how you filled my soul
every single day with constant
bliss, reminding me I never had
to endure a heartache alone again

I could write these words, but I fear
if I let them escape me I'll have
nothing left
*from the beautiful side of our love.*

# Writer's Block

I often wonder if anything in my
life will give me as much possibility
as I believed you would

Are there more beautiful words that I
will find that can compare to this
new vocabulary you've given me?

And when you're nothing but
a distant memory,
will I still have it inside of me
to want to learn a whole new language?

I could find myself going backward
down this writer's block
like I have often wandered
back through familiar streets
waiting for a past love to knock on my door

But why would I go back
when there are too many roads to travel
and too many maps to explore?
Why would I now stop believing that
opportunity will come knocking once more?

I know you are gone,
but what is meant for me won't pass me by
These words will not escape through an open window
at the first sign of sunshine

Sometimes I think things will leave me
because that fear has often come true
but the words will stay with me
through the darker times, much unlike you

# Cuckoo

This awakened soul
is nothing more than lost love
collecting its toll

—

*We are all born into this flawed world.*
*This world full of people who don't understand where we came*
*from*
*or what we've been through.*

*People will be cruel to us because it's a lot easier than taking*
*the time to understand all the tortured pieces of our minds.*

*You can blame these people for making you hate the world*
*and keep yourself hidden from the parts of it*
*that might break you again,*

*Or you can accept that these things are a part of life and make*
*the choice to be happy with the only one you're given.*

# The Same Words

If you want
people to turn
the page you
need to stop
writing the
same words
over and
over and
over again

# Punctuation

Don't cry, baby
Don't, crybaby

Don't be fooled by
the letters you see

Sometimes it's better
to look in between

—

You can't put band-aids over insecurities
You can't put band-aids over insecurities
You can't put band-aids over insecurities

but it hurts
I know it hurts

# Stop Trying to be Perfect

Every time you run towards perfection
You're running in the wrong direction

# Right Place, Right Time

You'll know when
place and time
are perfectly aligned
because you'll hear
them softly whisper,
"You're right where
you belong."

# Aurora

I thought your light
was there to guide me
and tell me where to go;
illuminating the space
for me to call my home

But even though I
couldn't see it, my
electricity lit up
the sky; I just had
to leave that home
and finally step
outside

# Values

I fell in love with your values
But you failed to see the value in me

# Yard Work

You see the green grass on the other side
but I see the rake, fertilizer, lawn mower,
hose, seeds, shears, gardening gloves,
watering can, shovel, wheelbarrow, and
pitchfork.

You can't just pick up a hoe, and expect
to grow vegetables.

# What Once Was

It's funny to think
What once occupied your mind
Is a life and a future
You had to leave behind
You jump to the memories
You never thought would end
From a companion and lover
To not even a friend

—

*Maybe we forget things when we drink because those aren't the moments worth remembering. Because life wants us to know that everything is better in moderation, and when we ingest too much too quickly, we are missing out on something so much more important.*

*We try to cram so much feeling into our lives all at once as if getting plastered and feeling high is going out of style, and love comes along in one passing opportunity.*

*But maybe we need to enjoy the slower parts of life. The years of loneliness where we happily wait for the perfect boy to appear around the corner. The nights of heartbreak where we pour all of our emotions out so that afterward, we almost feel indestructible.*

*Maybe these are the moments worth remembering*
*Not because we miraculously took on everything all at once— but because these are the moments that showed us how to.*

# Born On Fire

We were born on fire
And had to learn to be cool
But you don't learn
From following the rules

# Flaming Hearts

We were so much alike
so much burning passion
in two hearts

But you can't put out
fire with fire, and you
never wanted to burn

# The Nitty Gritty

I feel bad for you since you won't excel
Just doing what you do so well
Acting tough and sitting pretty
But to get what you want
You have to dig through
The nitty gritty

# The Finish Line

You're so young and
yet you put the finish
line right at your feet

I feel sorry you'll
have so many years
of nothingness to
run towards

# Long Gone

There were so many hurdles
But I was persistent
I wanted you with me
But you took the path with less resistance

Maybe someday you'll come up and find me
But I think you are lost
And you're too far behind me

# A Muse

I looked good as your muse
And good on your arm
But I wasn't born to amuse
I was born to take charge

# Perception

You'll look for me in every woman
But not find one who's quite as driven

They'll love your hair, your lips, your face
But looks do not take passion's place

Perfection is perception of the mind
And love like ours is hard to find

# Tough Love

You think I don't have
The capacity to understand
But when I'm not blinded
By the love of a man
No matter how broken
I pick myself up
Because if there's one thing
I've always known
It's the meaning
Of tough love

—

*Learning to love yourself while learning to love another is possible when you know your limits and don't let anyone tell you they need more of you than you are able to give them*

# Closure

There's no such thing as closure
Only openness
Because when you're truly ready
To end one chapter
It means you are willing
To open another

# I Carry You With Me

I always think about us
Trying to remember what was real
Recalling moments of temptation
That I'd forgotten how to feel
Now only lessons linger
I won't ever let them go
I carry pieces of you with me
They help to make me whole

# Until We Meet Again

We spoke again on that perfect day,
after all the anger blew away.

"Maybe we'll meet again," he said.
He wanted the old me,
but the old me
was dead.

# Reality Check

It was fun to make believe
that you were really right for me
But acceptance taught me
Beauty lies where you place it
And reality is easier
Whenever you face it

# I Left Him in the Past

It has been years since I saw him.
He was once everything to me,
And I always wondered
if we'd ever meet again

I knew I was a better woman
and I was eager to see the man he became
When I opened my mouth to show him
how much I've grown
He silenced me and said,
"You haven't changed a bit."
That's when I knew
he was exactly where I left him

—

While I was grateful
for every man I ever loved,
and every lesson I ever learned,
what I have been most grateful for
is my heart.

Because through all the pain it endured,
it would never settle for anything less
than what it would give

# You Broke Me Open

And after all is said and done they asked me,
"Why did you love him?
He abandoned you because he couldn't figure out how to love
He left you because he didn't want the responsibility
He made you feel worthless
because he wanted someone to blame."

I know how he made me feel and that he could've been better
But all I could say was,
"Because he never abandoned me.
He simply set me free."

You have found the back of my book.
You have opened me and
flipped through my pages, and here you are. At the end.
Take a deep breath.

We have met at the perfect time.
After life has been a little cruel and somehow
strangely beautiful.
But here you are,
and I hope you have found something
other than the back of this book.

Thank you. Thank you for reading these words,
I wanted so badly to share them with you.
I am thankful that you decided to pick up these pages.

We struggle so frequently to pick up our broken pieces
Yet, you continued to flip through all of mine
and I hope each page has cut into you in a unique way

Somehow your life has led you to find these pages.
Not everything in life proves it can last,
but you turned each page with the intent to get
right to this exact moment.

No matter how hard it was to get here,
or where you have come from, you made it.
I am so grateful that you made it here.

Somehow, something made you want to open me up.
I am glad you did, but now I want to know how you are.
How are you?
It's strange to do introductions at the end,

but I hope you can open up to me a bit more now.
After all, you did have your hands all over me.

Take a deep breath. Enjoy this moment,
because it's not really the end, is it?

I hope you are feeling something wonderful
like how I felt writing these words
and how I feel right now. In this moment.
There are darker pages in me,
but each page brings a feeling of something new
and that is wonderful, isn't it?

I carry the weight of these pages more lightly now
and I hope you feel lighter too
and I hope you feel like
there is nothing too heavy for you to carry

Take a deep breath
Take these moments with you
Take these pages with you if you would like
They are for you.

Everything in your life is for you, and you are now part of
my life.
You are part of life's beautiful plan,
and somehow that plan led you here.

So thank you
I really can't thank you enough
for being here

# About the Author

Brynn Taylor's writing first started to gain popularity when her articles *Why Being An Outgoing Introvert is So Much Harder Than People Realize* and *This is Why I'm Single (and No, I Don't Want You)* were published by Thought Catalog in 2016. Today, her work can be seen in Thought Catalog, Elite Daily, and on her blog, Brynnspiration.com. Find Brynn on Twitter @brynnspire, Instagram @brynnspiration_, and on Facebook at facebook.com/brynnspire.

## YOU MIGHT ALSO LIKE:

*All The Words I Should Have Said*
by Rania Naim

*But Before You Leave*
by Kirsten Corley

*She Who Destroys the Light*
by Shahida Arabi

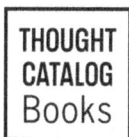

THOUGHT
CATALOG
Books

# THOUGHT CATALOG

### IT'S A WEBSITE.
www.thoughtcatalog.com

### SOCIAL
facebook.com/thoughtcatalog
twitter.com/thoughtcatalog
tumblr.com/thoughtcatalog
instagram.com/thoughtcatalog

### CORPORATE
www.thought.is

www.ingramcontent.com/pod-product-compliance
Lightning Source LLC
Chambersburg PA
CBHW031623040426
42452CB00007B/647